SONATAS FOR VIOLIN SOLO AND
VIOLONCELLO WITH CEMBALO

Recent Researches in the Music of the Baroque Era is one of four quarterly series (Middle Ages and Early Renaissance; Renaissance; Baroque Era; Pre-Classical, Classical, and Early Romantic Eras) which make public the early music that is being brought to light in the course of current musicological research.

Each volume is devoted to works by a single composer or in a single genre of composition, chosen because of their potential interest to scholars and performers, and prepared for publication according to the standards that govern the making of all reliable historical editions.

Subscribers to this series, as well as patrons of subscribing institutions, are invited to apply for information about the "Copyright-Sharing Policy" of A-R Editions, Inc., under which the contents of this volume may be reproduced free of charge for performance use.

Correspondence should be addressed:

A-R Editions, Inc.
152 West Johnson Street
Madison, Wisconsin 53703

RECENT RESEARCHES IN THE MUSIC OF THE BAROQUE ERA · VOLUME XX

Giovanni Antonio Piani

SONATAS FOR VIOLIN SOLO AND VIOLONCELLO WITH CEMBALO

Edited by Barbara Garvey Jackson

A-R EDITIONS, INC. · MADISON

© 1975, A-R Editions, Inc.

For Kern

Contents

Preface	vii
Opus I	
Sonata I in G minor	1
Sonata II in E minor	9
Sonata III in F major	22
Sonata IV in G major	30
Sonata V in B-flat major	49
Sonata VI in G major	59
Sonata VII in C minor	68
Sonata VIII in B minor	77
Sonata IX in A minor	88
Sonata X in D major	97
Sonata XI in E-flat major	105
Sonata XII in A major	113

Preface

THE COMPOSER

Little is known about the life of Giovanni Antonio Piani (*dit* Desplanes). He was born in 1678 into a family of Neapolitan musicians whose name is variously spelled *Piana*, *Piano*, and *Piani*. His father, Pietro Giacomo Piani of Bologna, moved to Naples in 1674 to take a post as court trumpeter. In 1676 Pietro married a Genoese girl, Anna Caterina Drue, who was the mother of Giovanni Antonio Piani and his brother, Bartolomeo. Anna Caterina apparently died sometime prior to 1698, for in that year Pietro married a Neapolitan girl named Anna Piscina who bore him two more sons, Girolamo and Gennaro.

All of Pietro's sons were musicians. Bartolomeo (1684–1748) studied trumpet at the *Conservatorio della Pietà dei Turchini* and, like his father, became a court trumpeter. Girolamo (1703–1756) was a trumpeter who also sang *basso buffo* at the *Teatro dei Fiorentini* and later in Palermo, Venice, and Rome. In 1736, Girolamo joined the Royal Chapel in Naples as a bass; later, he played trumpet in the *Teatro San Carlo* orchestra, as well. Gennaro (1709–1781) was a horn player in the orchestras of the San Bartolomeo and San Carlo theaters, as well as in the Royal Chapel. He taught wind instruments for forty-four years at the *Conservatorio della Pietà dei Turchini*.[1]

Giovanni Antonio Piani studied violin in 1691 at the *Conservatorio della Pietà dei Turchini* with Vinciprova and Cailò. It is not known where Piani was between 1691 and 1704, but in 1704 he was in France in the service of Louis Alexandre de Bourbon (Count of Toulouse, Grand Admiral of France, and recently legitimatized natural son of Louis XIV and Madame de Montespan). From 1720–1760, Piani was in the employ of the Imperial Court Chapel in Vienna, where he was the most highly paid instrumentalist.[2] According to La Laurencie he was Senalliè's teacher, though Van der Straeten questions this tradition.[3] Fétis stated that he settled in Venice sometime before 1738, citing a story from the *Mercure de France* of 1738 to the effect that he had been convicted of forgery and condemned to have his head cut off.[4] This was, however, a false story, retracted in the same paper in August of 1738.[5] La Laurencie's mistaken identifications of Piani as a Venetian may be based on the Fétis article.[6] There is no reliable evidence that he was in Venice at all while he was on the paylist of the Imperial Court in Vienna.

After the accession of Maria Theresa in 1741, the total number of musicians was reduced and the salaries of those remaining in the Imperial Chapel at Vienna were lowered. At this time, Piani's salary was cut from the 1800 guilders which he had received yearly since 1721 to 1200 guilders. Even so, Piani remained the most highly paid instrumentalist.

Other violinists of note in the court during Piani's years there included Nicola Matteis, the younger, and Angelo Ragazzi. One Carlo Tomaso (Tommaso) Piani, employed by the Imperial Chapel in Vienna from 1717 until his death at the age of 76 on May 25, 1760, was probably a cousin of Giovanni Antonio (his father's brother's son). Carlo Tomaso had been a student of Cailò at the *Conservatorio della Pietà dei Turchini* until 1705, and his presence in Vienna may have had something to do with Giovanni Antonio's decision to go there.[7]

THE MUSIC

None of Giovanni Antonio Piani's works survives except for the twelve violin sonatas of Opus 1, published in Paris in 1712. A ten-year privilege (copyright) was granted on May 29, 1712, to "Jean Antoine Piani dit Desplanes" to publish "various works of music, both vocal and instrumental, of his composition"; no other reference to vocal music survives.[8]

The Amsterdam firm of Roger and Le Cene issued Piani's twelve sonatas in 1716. The six sonatas Piani had specified in his Paris edition as being for either flute or violin were published under Roger's imprint as *VI. Sonate a Flauto e Basso Continuo*; this volume was listed in the publisher's catalogue as number 190.[9] Roger and Le Cene then issued two volumes of violin sonatas numbered 190 and 191 in their catalogue.[10] The first of these volumes contained the six "flute sonatas," re-issued as violin music; apparently, only the title page was changed. The second volume consisted of the remaining six sonatas of Piani's Opus 1. The Roger and Le Cene edition of Piani's sonatas was consulted extensively in the preparation of the present volume.[11] However, the principal source of this edition is the Paris print of 1712. Discrepancies between the present edition and the editions published in Paris and Amsterdam are discussed in the Critical Notes.

Although the privilege granted Piani in 1712 was for a period of ten years, no later works seem to have been printed. No publications or manuscripts from the Vienna period are known. However, there apparently was a continuing interest in Piani's music in mid-century Paris; a twenty-year privilege was granted to Charles Nicholas Le Clerc on November 13, 1750, for the printing of instrumental works by Desplanes (Piani), Locatelli, Lanzetti, Maho, and other important composers of the first half of the century.[12] No extant publications by Le Clerc include any works by Piani.

The twelve sonatas of Opus 1 are mentioned in histories of violin music because they contain the first known markings of *crescendo, diminuendo,* and *messa di voce,* and because they are the first sources which give fingerings for the second position for the violin in printed music. Although these dynamic markings and innovative fingerings, as well as a wealth of detailed bowings and careful indications of ornamentation, are found in Piani's sonatas, no detailed study of the performance practice indicated in the works has ever been published, and none of the sonatas has previously been available in a modern edition.

NOTES ON PERFORMANCE

Dynamics

Visually, the most striking feature of these sonatas is the use of solid wedges to show *crescendo, diminuendo,* and *messa di voce* (◀━▶). Solid wedges appear in the works of Veracini and Geminiani somewhat later, but neither of these composers used them in the same way Piani did. The opening wedge (◀) appears in the slow movements of almost all of Piani's sonatas; it is also seen occasionally in faster movements such as *allemandas,* and once in a *corrente* (Sonata III, p. 26, m.59). The *crescendo* is always used either on a single note of long value tied to a note of shorter value or on a dotted note. Usually, the harmony changes on the dot or on the strong beat into which the note is tied. A dissonant chord (usually a $^6_5$) or a suspension is often found at the end of a *crescendo.* A case in which the *crescendo* wedge is used without dissonance is found in the *Allemanda* of Sonata IV (p. 37, mm.25–27). In one instance, the opening wedge is combined with a trill (Sonata IV, p. 30, m.3).

The closing wedge (▶) is used rarely. When it does appear, it is at phrase endings that are followed without pause by the opening of a new phrase (*Poco andante,* Sonata XII, p.119, solo, m.18). The closing wedge also occurs in a very affective passage in the *Sarabanda* of Sonata II (p.14, solo, m.19), creating a sigh at the end of a phrase.

The opening and closing wedge (━━━ *messa di voce—crescendo* and *diminuendo*) usually appears on long notes without chord change and is sometimes an affective rendering of isolated notes (*Sarabanda,* Sonata III, p.27, solo, mm.14–15). In one instance, it is applied to very long notes in the solo and bass parts; although the bass participates in the *crescendo* portion of the nuance, the effect of the closing part of the wedge is cut off by rests in the bass (*Adagio,* Sonata IV, p.39, mm.32–37). There are no specific markings for *crescendi* or *diminuendi* covering more than one note.

Piani also uses the terms *dolce* and *forte* to indicate dynamics in longer sections. Quiet codas are formed by marking the closing phrases of many movements *dolce;* and one movement, the *Sarabanda* of Sonata II, is even marked *dolce assai.* Some closing sections are marked *dolce,* changing to *forte* for the last few measures; these dynamic indications suggest that the real intent was to create a section beginning *dolce* and increasing to *forte.* Often in the sonatas (*Allemanda* of Sonata II, p.12, mm.25–26), the *dolce* and *forte* markings clearly indicate real echo dynamics, sometimes with varied embellishment. Most of the terrace dynamics move from *forte* to *dolce,* but at the end of the *Siciliana* of Sonata VI, a *dolce* phrase is repeated *forte.*

One surprising aspect of both dynamic and articulation markings is the distinction sometimes made between what is indicated in the violin part and what is indicated in the bass part. In the *Allemanda* of Sonata I, the concluding section is marked *Vln. sempre dolce, B° sempre forte.* The *Preludios* of Sonatas IV and VII specify that the violin part is *affettuoso* and that the bass is *staccato.* In both sonatas, there are embellishments for the violin with dotted note patterns in the bass (they might well be played with over-dotting). The *Allegro assai* of Sonata IV is marked *sempre forte* in the bass at the beginning and proceeds throughout the movement in *staccato.* The violin part, on the other hand, has some contrasting sections marked *dolce.* Perhaps the most astonishing marking in the bass is the opening wedge *crescendo* accompanying the long *messa di voce* in Sonata IV, mentioned above. This, of course, could only be done by the melodic bass played on the cello.

Fingerings

The care with which Piani marked special problems did not stop with the dynamics. In two movements, the *Siciliana* of Sonata III (p.28, mm.15–16) and the *Corrente* of Sonata V (p.53, m.37), he gives fingerings for brief passages in the second position which are probably the earliest-known printed fingerings for that position. In the *Allemanda* of Sonata XII (p.115, m.11 and p.118, m.76) he indicates the fourth finger rather than the open string in a first-position passage. Double-stemmed notes are used in a few places to indicate a unison stopped note on one string doubled by the next open string.

Tempo and character markings

Piani's tempo markings are quite descriptive. Clearly, his favorite word was *affettuoso:* markings like *largo, et affettuoso; poco allegro, et affettuoso;* and *larghetto, et affettuoso* are found in every sonata. *Allegro* is commonly *mà non presto,* although there is one *allegro assai. Spiccato* (eighteenth-century meaning is "detached," and does not indicate a particular bowing) and *staccato* are marked at the beginning of five movements in the twelve sonatas of Opus 1. *Spiccato* is used when both violin and bass parts are playing in a detached style, while *staccato* is the indication for the bass when it is using an articulation contrasting with that of the violin. Both indications are mainly associated with dotted rhythm patterns. In

Sonata VII, which has surprising mixtures of dotted rhythms and triplets, the term *spiccato* seems to indicate that the dotted rhythms are very detached, probably over-dotted, and not absorbed by the triplet patterns. Markings of *spiccato* and *staccato* are not Piani's only means of showing detached notes, as will be shown below.

Articulation and bowing

The affective character of the sonatas often calls for expressive separation between short motives, between sections, or even within phrases. In Sonata IX, a special mark is used for this sort of separation in both the *Preludio* and the *Grave:*

Sonata IX, *Preludio*, m.11

Short, impassioned motives, set off by rests, occur in some slow movements. In the *Sarabanda* of Sonata II (p.14, mm.17–20) rests and dynamic signs are combined to enhance the breathless character of the music. Expressive rests within phrases sometimes occur under a slur sign, as in the *Sarabanda* of Sonata VIII (p.82, m.9).

Piani uses a wide spectrum of bowings; he calls particular attention to three patterns using detached bowings in his famous preface (see Plate II).

The *notes égales, articulées, et un peu detachées* are staccato eighth-notes, used mainly in *allegro* movements. These three patterns are not *sautillé*; they would be played with the bowing now called *spiccato*.[13] They are found in the violin parts of the *Aria allegro* of Sonata X, the *Corrente* of Sonata V, and the bass parts of the *Andante* of Sonata X and *Allegro assai* of Sonata IV. Although not specifically marked, the unslurred eighth-notes of the *Allegro* of Sonata VII clearly have the same character (*notes égales, articulées, et un peu detachées*) and should be played *spiccato*.

Notes égales are commonly indicated by staccato dots in French practice, and it is clear that Piani used them in this way. The *Andante* of Sonata X has *égales staccato* bass notes; the slurred, stepwise pairs of eighth-notes in the violin part are *notes inégales*.

Piani's *avertissement* gives an example of a spectacular twelve-note, grouped staccato. This was probably played with lifted bows (the modern equivalent would be *flying staccato*), although nothing is specified as to whether the articulation was to be performed on or off the string. Grouped staccato notes occur only in descending scale passages (either *forte* or *dolce*) of rapid movements such as the *Corrente* of Sonata III and the *Allegro assai* of Sonata IV. The *Corrente* of Sonata XI is a firey movement in which the syncopation of the main motive is greatly enhanced by the use of grouped staccato notes and other brilliant bowings.

In the *avertissement* (see Plate II), Piani writes that a diversity of bowings gives his *gigas* a distinctive character; he illustrates several possible ways of bowing the groups of three eighth-notes which are often found in these dance movements:

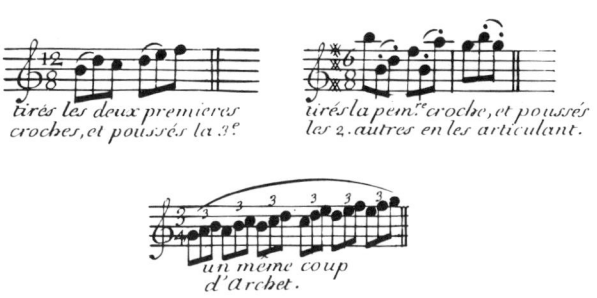

Piani's *gigas* fall into two categories. There are *affettuoso gigas* which use the bowing pattern ♩♩ and brilliant *gigas* which use many ♫♫ ♫♫ patterns (the grouped staccato notes should be played with lifted up-bows) and usually have a greater diversity of bowings. The *Gigas* of Sonatas I and IX are of the *affettuoso* type, while those of Sonatas II, VIII, XI, and XII are brilliant. Although the final *Allegro* of Sonata X is not so labeled, it is really a *giga affettuoso*; it has many slurred triplet patterns and is a movement in which the dotted-eighth plus sixteenth-note pattern should conform to the triplet rhythm.

The effectiveness of the bowings in the *allemandas* rarely involves grouped staccatos. Instead, the bowings exploit varying lengths and patterns of slurred groups, as in the following examples:

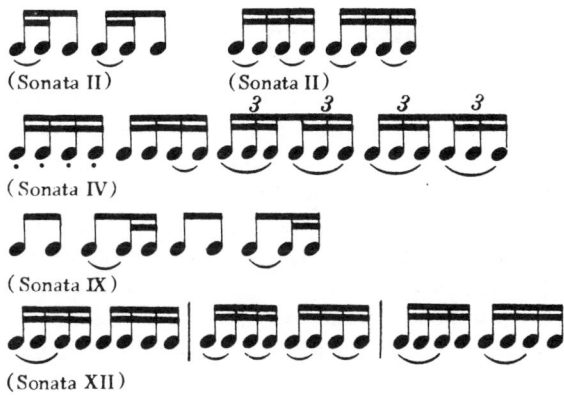

Sonata VIII does have grouped staccato for convenience in the slur lengths and bow direction of the rest of the pattern:

One unusual sign used by Piani is a long, undulating line found over very long groups of notes; there are often normal slurs over some groups of notes within the span of the longer line:

The meaning of this sign is not explained; it could be a long phrase marking or it might indicate a bowing of the *louré* type with gentle pulsations denoting groupings within the slur.

Ornaments[14]

The ornament signs used by Piani include the *pincé*, (') which he marks with a straight stroke, the trill which is always marked ✛, the slide (*coulé sur une tierce*) which is indicated either with a slash or with small notes, as shown:

and *appoggiaturas, port de voix* and other such ornaments indicated by small notes. His notation of small-note ornaments is very inconsistent in its use of slurs. One may find either ♪♩ or ♪♩ . No consistent pattern seems to govern the choice between notation with or without a slur, and it is likely that the performer did not distinguish between them.

Both slow and fast movements are quite ornamented; all ornaments, other than those mentioned above, are written out fully. Ornaments in the bass part are normally indicated by a cross and are usually trills.

EDITORIAL PRACTICE

As stated above, the print of the Sonatas made in Paris (1712) is the principal source of the present edition. The Roger and Le Cene edition (Amsterdam, 1716) of Piani's Sonatas was also consulted. The copy of the Paris edition which was used is in the Library of Congress. The two-volume Roger and Le Cene edition is found in the Bibliothèque Nationale.

Piani's spellings and accent markings are inconsistent; they never have a stylistic significance but have been retained as a matter of curiosity. However, his use of Italian spellings for dance names is uniform; on the one occasion when he wishes to have a French-style *courante*, he labels it *Corrente alla Francese*.

Notation of accidentals has been made consistent with modern practice. Redundant accidentals have been eliminated by the editor. Accidentals placed in square brackets are not marked in the source but are added by the editor to eliminate uncertainties as to the duration of accidentals or to correct errors in the source. Cautionary accidentals placed in parentheses are added by the editor to make clear the limited influence of certain original accidentals.

Piani's figured bass practice is fairly consistent and standard, although he sometimes uses ♯ and ♮ interchangeably for raised notes whose accidental would be ♮. The figured bass symbols used in this edition are taken from the Paris source. Special signs used in the Amsterdam edition are as follows: 7̄ (flatted seventh), 5̸ (diminished fifth). The Paris edition reflects Piani's use of 5̸ to indicate a diminished fifth. He explains the sign in his *avertissement*, although it is not an uncommon usage. The sign has been retained in the present edition.

Where old "modal" key signs (such as one flat for G minor) were used, the key signature has been modernized. Modal key signatures have been modernized in Sonatas I, VII, XI, and XII. The Critical Notes for each of these sonatas describe the original signatures.

Inexact rhythm notation often occurs in rapid note groups following dotted notes. Piani's notation has been retained in such cases, since the use of a modern regularization might give the false impression that a mathematically correct division of the beat was intended. A common pattern is ♩. ♫ in which neither the effect of a triplet rhythm ♫ nor the fussy exactness of ♫ is appropriate.

Piani's inconsistent use of slurs in appoggiaturas and similar small-note ornaments has been retained. His signs for *pincé* and trill have been replaced by modern signs: *pincé* as ✛ and trill as ~. The cross has been retained as the ornament sign in the bass part. The long wavy slurs, described above, have been retained in their original form in this edition.

Dynamic signs have been changed from solid wedges to modern notation: <, >, and <>. Their placement and the restriction of their use to single notes has been retained. Piani's terms for dynamic levels, *dolce* and *forte* (in modern usage, *piano* and *forte*), have been retained in this edition.

The realization of movements which may involve rhythmic conventions of *notes inégales*, over-dotting of ♫ rhythms, or the interpretation of dotted rhythms as triplets has been made to agree with the original notation of the rhythm of the bass part. The performer is, therefore, free to treat such realizations in accordance with the conventions he decides should apply to the passage in question. In a few places, such as the interpretation of ♪♫ as ♪.♫, suggestions have been made above the part (see p.9, solo, m.6); some suggestions about specific movements have been made in the course of this introduction. However, the intent of the realization is that the performer should have visible to him a notation as close to that of the original as is practical. The performer should treat all parts, including the editor's realization, with the stylistic freedoms and conventions appropriate to Parisian (and Italian) music of this period.

Piani, though Italian, clearly made use of many French conventions in his music. He also suggests in the *avertissement* (see Plate II) that his symbols, such as those for dynamics, were neither completely new nor unique. Piani considered it necessary to give an explanation of the symbols "so that those who do not know their use can execute" the sonatas according to his intention. Evidently, there must have been some musicians in Paris who did know their use, but we do not know who they were.

CRITICAL NOTES

Although the present edition is based primarily on the Paris source, the Amsterdam edition of Roger and Le Cene was consulted extensively, also. These notes refer to discrepancies between the present edition and the earlier editions published in Paris and in Amsterdam. A = Amsterdam edition, and P = Paris edition. If no edition is indicated, the note refers to both. Page and measure numbers refer to the full score rather than to the solo part-book for violin. The usual system of pitch designation is used wherein middle c is c', two-line c is c'', and so forth.

Sonata I—P.1: Original key signature contained b'-flat. *Preludio:* p.2, m.12, bass, final note, ornament present in P, only. *Allemanda:* p.2, m.6, vn., notes 2–3, slur present in A, only; p.5, m.84, vn., notes 1–4, slurs present in P, only. *Giga:* p.7, m.35, bass, note 1, P has natural-3 in figured bass; p.7, m.35, bass, note 2, A has ♭$^6_3$ in figured bass.

Sonata II—*Sarabanda:* p.15, mm.27–28, vn., slurs present in these measures in P, only. Piani seems to be very inconsistent in his use of the slur with the appoggiatura, so this is probably never a significant matter in these sonatas. *Giga:* p.16, m.41, vn., note 4, staccato dot present in P, only. It is not used consistently in P, although it does echo the pattern of m.39 where the dot also appears. P.18, m.71, *Volti* (turn) is used for several page-turns in the sonatas, but here *Volti presto,* coming at the end of the movement, indicates that the next movement should be as soon as possible. He sometimes uses *Volti presto* or even *Volti prestissimo* for bad page-turns in mid-movement. *Presto:* p.20, m.64, vn., notes 3 and 5 are d'' in A; p.21, m.89, vn., notes 3 and 4 are dotted eighth and sixteenth in P.

Sonata III—*Sarabanda:* p.26, m.2, bass, note 2, sharp omitted in figured bass in A; p.27, m.16, vn., note 1, trill on this note in A, only.

Sonata IV—*Allemanda:* p.35, m.7, vn., notes 9–20, sixteenth-note triplets are consistently notated as thirty-second-notes. *Allegro assai:* p.42, m.45, vn., notes 1–2, tie is present in P, only; p.45, m.118, bass, note 1, P has flat-3 in figured bass, here.

Sonata V—*Largo:* p.56, the word "segue" found at the end of this movement in the score is spelled "siegue" in the source. *Giga:* p.57, m.9, vn., notes 5–6, slur over these notes present in A, only.

Sonata VII—P.68, the original key signature contained b'-flat and e''-flat. *Allegro, é spiccato:* p.74, m.9, bass, note 1, figured bass is 5; p.76, m.67, bass, note 2, natural in figured bass is present in A, only.

Sonata VIII—*Allemanda:* p.79, m.3, vn., final note is g''.

Sonata IX–*Preludio:* p.88, m.11, vn., note 7 is written as a dotted quarter. *Giga:* p.96, m.30, vn., note 1 is a quarter-note instead of a dotted quarter-note.

Sonata X—*Aria:* p.101, m.23, vn., note 4, slide is present in A, only.

Sonata XI—P.105, the original key signature contained b'-flat and e''-flat. *Grave:* p. 105, m.10, bass, note 4, figured bass is $^6_3$ in A; p.106, m.13, bass, note 6, figured bass has a flat in A, and figured bass seventh is in P, only. *Corrente:* p.106, m.6, vn., notes 3–5, slur over notes 4 and 5, only, in A; p.107, m.34, vn., note 3 is b-flat in P. *Giga:* p.110, m.19, vn., all notes, a wavy line over the notes of this measure in P; p.111, m.39, vn., slur over notes 5–6 in A, only.

Sonata XII—P.113; original key signature contained f''-sharp and c''-sharp. *Preludio:* p.114, m.40, bass and vn., note 1, dot present in A, only; repeat sign missing. *Poco andante:* p.119, m.13, repeat sign present in A, only.

ACKNOWLEDGMENTS

The editor wishes to thank the Graduate Research Council of the University of Arkansas for a grant assisting in the completion of this edition. Thanks are also expressed to the Library of Congress for making available a xerox copy of the 1712 Paris edition of the sonatas, and to the Bibliothèque Nationale of Paris for making available a microfilm of the Roger and Le Cene Amsterdam edition. The editor appreciates the assistance of the Music Division on providing these plates.

Barbara Garvey Jackson
University of Arkansas

July, 1975

Notes

[1] Ulisse Prota-Giurleo, "Piana, (Piano, Piani)," *Sartori Enciclopedia della Musica* (Milan: Ricordi, 1964), pp.430–431. I am indebted to Neal Zaslaw of Cornell University for his assistance in bringing these articles to my attention.

[2] Ludwig Ritter von Köchel, *Die Kaiserliche Hof-musikkapelle in Wien von 1543 bis 1867 nach urkundlichen Forschungen* (Vienna: Hölder, 1869), pp.77, 83, 86; item numbers 925, 1068, 1145. His name is given as Jos. Ant. Piani in items #1068 and 1145.

[3] Lionel de La Laurencie, *L'École française de violon de Lully à Viotti; études d'histoire et d'esthétique* (3 vols.; Paris: Delagrave, 1922–24), Vol. I, p.191. E. van der Straeten, *The History of the Violin; Its Ancestors and Collatoral Instruments from Earliest Times* (London: Cassell & Co., 1933), Vol. II, p.16.

[4] F.J. Fétis, *Biographie universelle des musiciens*, 2nd ed. (Paris: 1860–65), Vol. III, p.6. Entry is under the name "Desplanes (Jean-Antoine Piani)."

[5] Van der Straeten, *op. cit.*, p.15.

[6] La Laurencie, *op. cit.*, p. 191, followed by David Boyden, *History of Violin Playing from its Origins to 1761 and its Relationship to the Violin and Violin Music* (London: Oxford University Press, 1965), p. 414.

[7] Ulisse Prota-Giurleo, *loc. cit.*; Köchel, *op. cit.*, pp.76, 83, 86, item numbers 924, 1069, 1146. According to Robert Eitner, Carlo Tomaso Piani served as violinist in the Bavarian Court Chapel before moving to Vienna in 1717. Robert Eitner, *Quellen-Lexicon der Muskier und Musikgelehrten* (Leipzig: Breitkopf & Härtel, 1902), Vol. VII, p.427. Eitner (p.428) says one other Piani is known, although no relationship with Giovanni Antonio has been established. This Piani was a violinist in the Court Chapel at Kassel in 1725.

[8] Michel Brenet, "La librarie musicale en France de 1653 à 1790 d'après les Registres de privilèges," *Sammelbände der Internationalen Musikgesellschaft*, Vol. VIII, p.423.

[9] These are, evidently, the flute sonatas referred to by J.G. Walther in the article on Piani in *Musikalisches Lexikon* (Leipzig: Wolfgang Deer, 1732), p.479.

[10] *Catalogue des livres de Musique, Imprimés à Amsterdam, chez Etienne Roger & continues par Michel Charles Le Cene*, (Amsterdam: Le Cene, 1716). #190, VI. Sonate a Flauto e Basso Continuo, p.316; #190, #191, XII. Sonate a violino solo, p.329.

[11] Giovanni Antonio Piani, *Sonate / a Violino sole è Violoncello col Cimbalo / Dedicate / All' Altezza Serenissima / Di / Lodovico Alessandro di Borbone / Duca di Penthievre, di Damville, de Château-Villain, e di Ramboüillet / Marchese d' Albert e&c./ Dá / Gio: An: Piani, detto Des Planes, Napolitano / Musico di Violino della sopra detta Altezza Serenissima / OPERA PRIMA / IN PARIGI / 1712.* (Copy in the Library of Congress).

Sonate / a Violino Solo è Violoncello col Cimbalo / di / Gio: Ant: Piani Des Planes / Musico di Camera di S. A. S. / Lodovico Alessandro di Borbone / Conte di Tolosa &c. &c. &c. / OPERA PRIMA / Libro Primo / Ces Six Sonates se peuvent aussi jouer sur les Flûtes / Amsterdam / Chez Estienne Roger & Le Cene Libraire / No. 190.

Sonate / a Violino Solo è Violoncello col Cimbalo / di / Gio: Ant: Piani Des Planes / Musico di Camera di S. A. S. / Lodovico Alessandro di Borbone / Conte di Tolosa &c. &c. &c. / OPERA PRIMA / Libro Secondo / Amsterdam / Chez Estienne Roger & Le Cene Librarie / No. 191. (Copies in the Bibliothèque Nationale).

[12] Brenet, *loc. cit.*

[13] La Laurencie, *op. cit.*, Vol.I, p.192; Boyden, *op. cit.*, p.414; and I (Barbara Garvey Seagrave and Joel Berman, *The A.S.T.A. Dictionary of Bowing Terms for String Instruments*, Urbana: American String Teachers Association, 1968, p.40) have all stated that Piani uses the term *sautillé* in his *avertissement*, and that his was the first use of the term. All of us were incorrect as the term does not appear, and the bowing example to which we were referring would not have been played *sautillé* then or now.

[14] For a more complete discussion of the performance of ornaments and of French rhythmic conventions of performance see Putnam Aldrich, "The Principal *Agréments* of the Seventeenth and Eighteenth Centuries: A Study in Musical Ornamentation" (Unpublished dissertation, Harvard University, 1942) and Newman Powell, "Rhythmic Freedom in the Performance of French Music from 1650 to 1735" (Unpublished dissertation, Stanford University, 1958), and Robert Donington, *The Interpretation of Early Music* (London: Faber and Faber, 2nd edition, 1973), and Robert Donington, *A Performer's Guide to Baroque Music* (New York: Charles Scribner's Sons, 1973).

Plate I. Piani, *Sonate a violino solo*—title page
Paris print, 1712 (Courtesy, Library of Congress)

Plate II. Piani, *Sonate a violino solo*—Avertissement
Paris print, 1712 (Courtesy, Library of Congress)

AVERTISSEMENT

I have thought that it was necessary to give an explanation here of some special symbols which are indicated in my book, so that those who do not know their use can execute my sonatas according to my intention.

This sign .... ◄— .... indicates that the bow stroke begins with sweetness and ends with force.

another .... —► .... which indicates that the bow stroke begins with force and ends dying away.

this one .... ◄—► .... indicates that one must begin with sweetness, strengthening the bow stroke in the middle, in accordance with the value of the note on which one encounters it, and ends with the same sweetness with which one began, so that one goes imperceptibly from one to the other.

equal notes, articulated and a little detached.

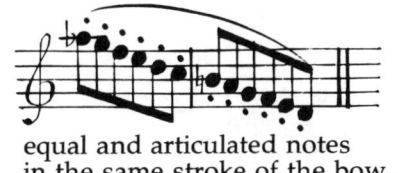

equal and articulated notes in the same stroke of the bow.

In the Gigue movements it is the diversity of the bow strokes which gives all the brilliance to the execution.

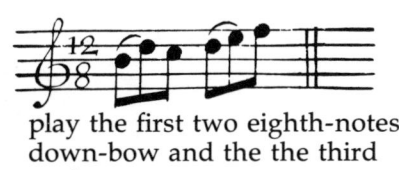

play the first two eighth-notes down-bow and the the third up-bow.

play the first eighth-note down-bow and the two others up-bow, articulating them.

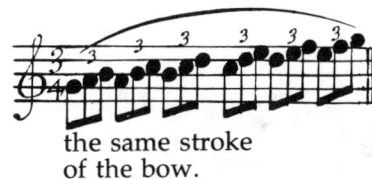

the same stroke of the bow.

down-bow. up-bow.

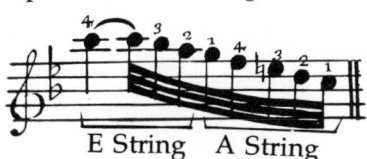

E String   A String

I have availed myself of these numbers for the transposition (shifting) of the fingers. See page 36.

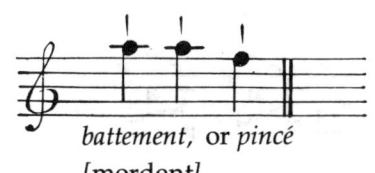

battement, or *pincé* [mordent]

diminished fifth ♭

There are six Sonatas in this book which one can play on the recorder and on the transverse flute, that is to say, the first, third, sixth, seventh, ninth, and tenth.

Plate III. Piani, *Sonate a violino solo*—Sonata I, Preludio
Paris print, 1712 (Courtesy, Library of Congress)

SONATAS FOR VIOLIN SOLO AND VIOLONCELLO WITH CEMBALO

Sonata I

Preludio

Largo, et affettuoso

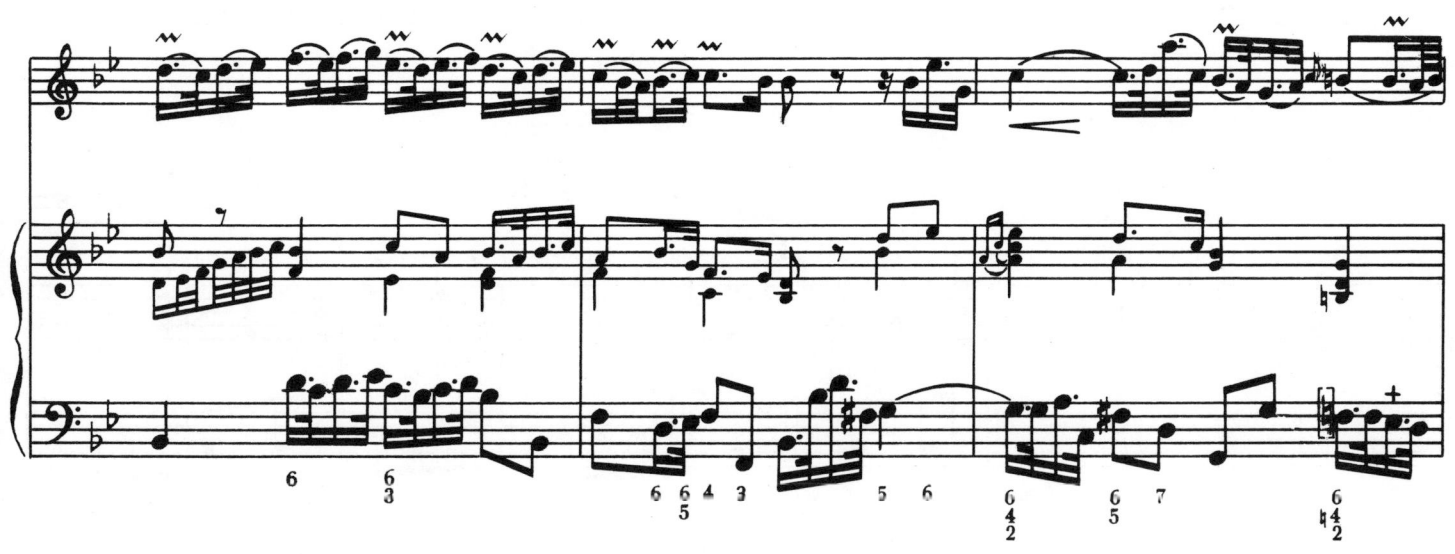

Allemanda
Allegro, ma non presto

Sarabanda
Largo, et affettuoso

Giga
Poco allegro, et affettuoso

Sonata II

Preludio
Poco andante

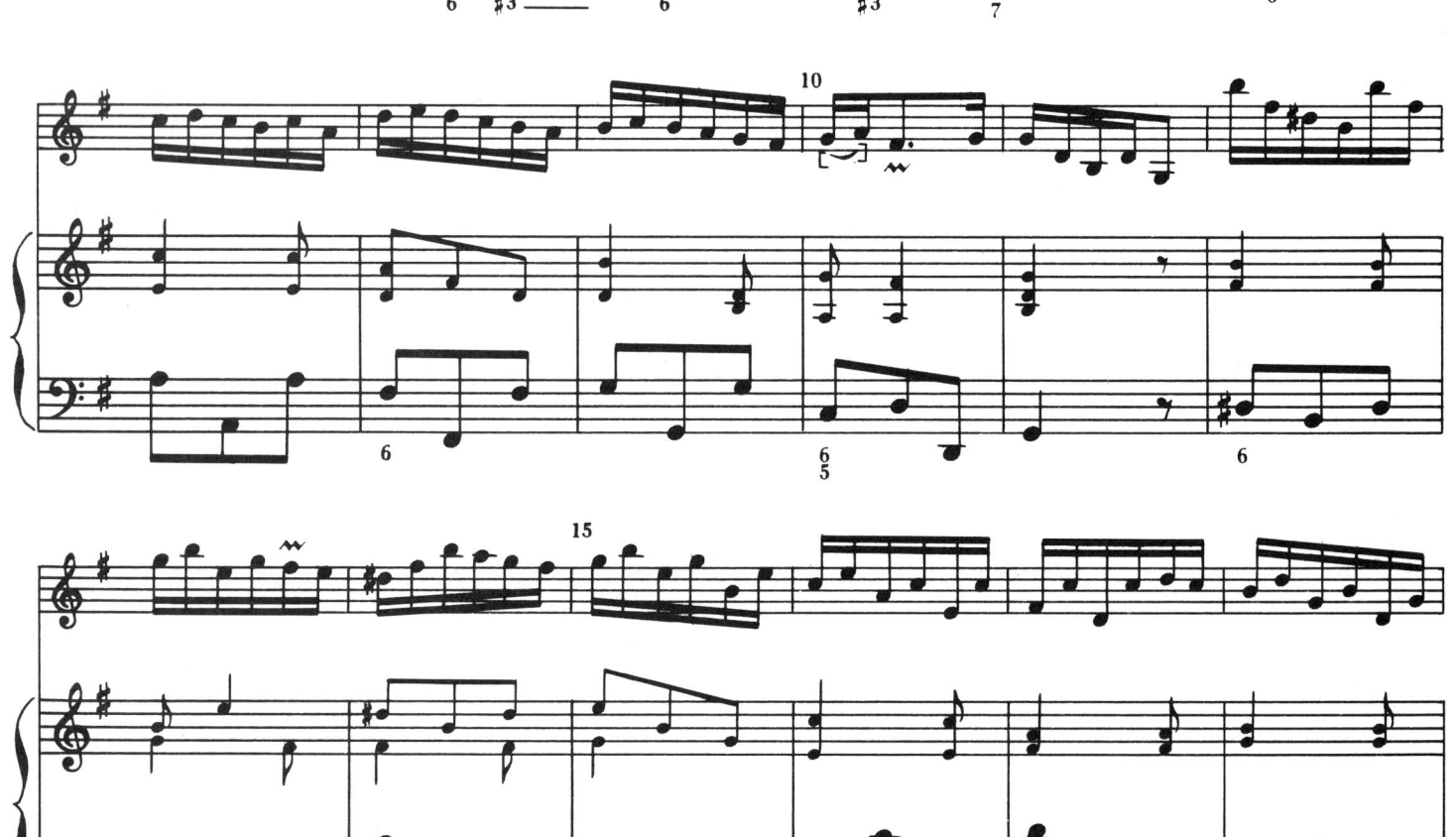

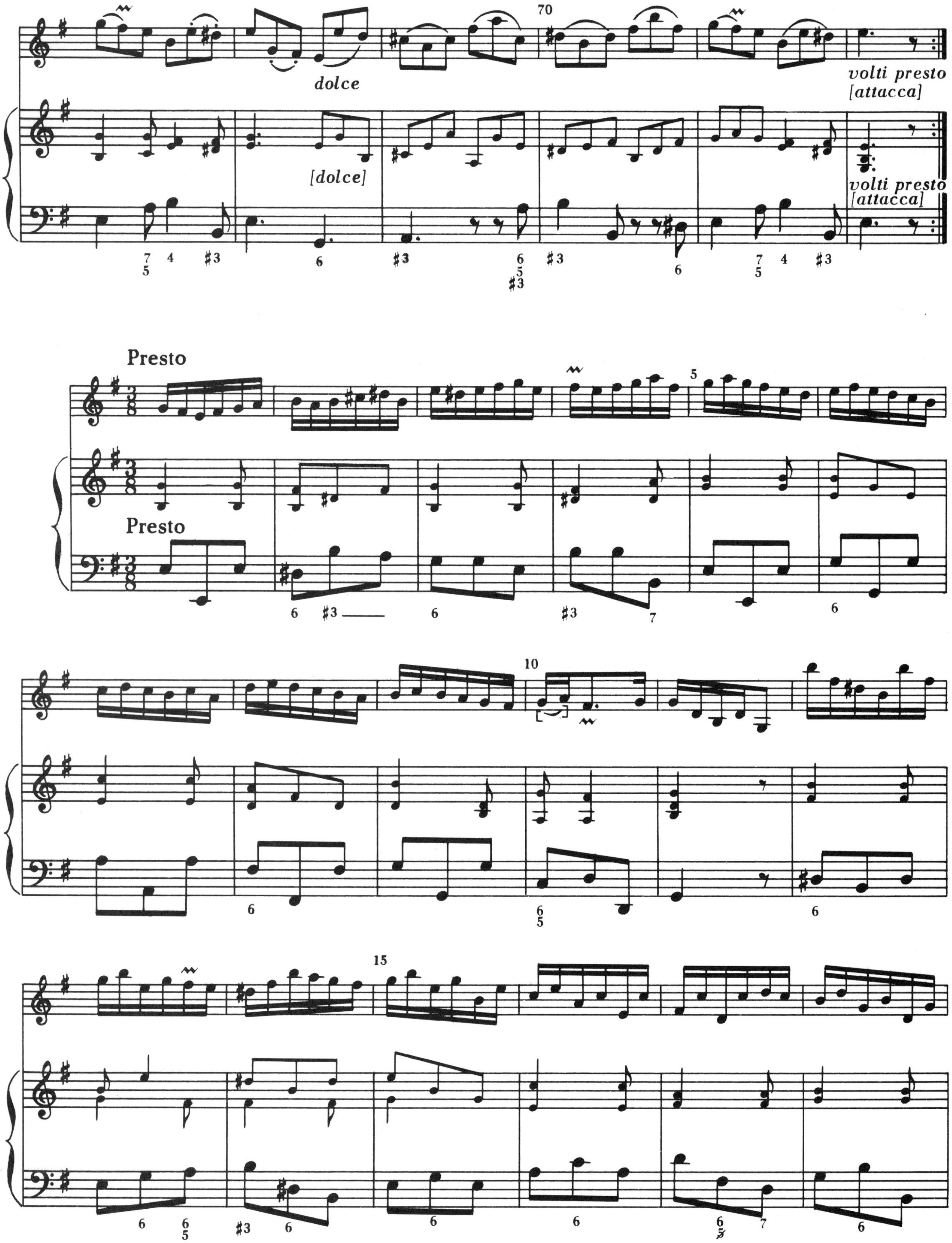
dolce
volti presto
[attacca]
[dolce]
volti presto
[attacca]
Presto
Presto

Sonata III

Preludio

Poco andante, et affettuoso

Corrente

Allegro, e spiccato

Siciliana
Larghetto, et affettuoso

Sonata IV

Preludio

Adagio, é affettuoso

Adagio, é staccato

Corrente

Allegro, mà non presto

Allemanda

Allegro mà non presto

40
dolce
[dolce]
Allegro assai
[R.H. legato]
Violino dolce
Allegro assai
[sempre staccato]
Basso sempre forte
5
10
forte
15

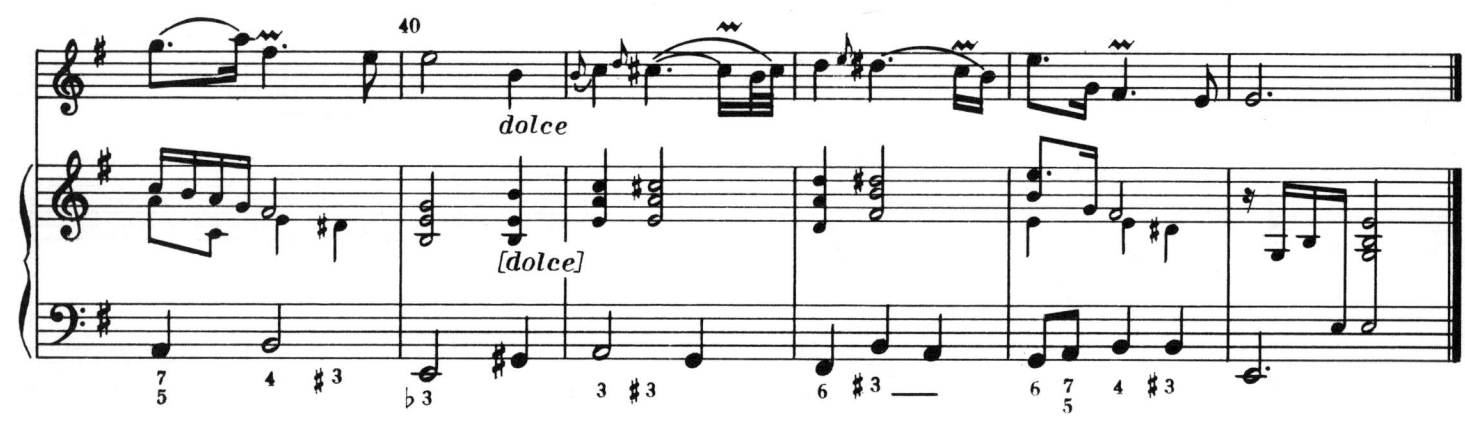

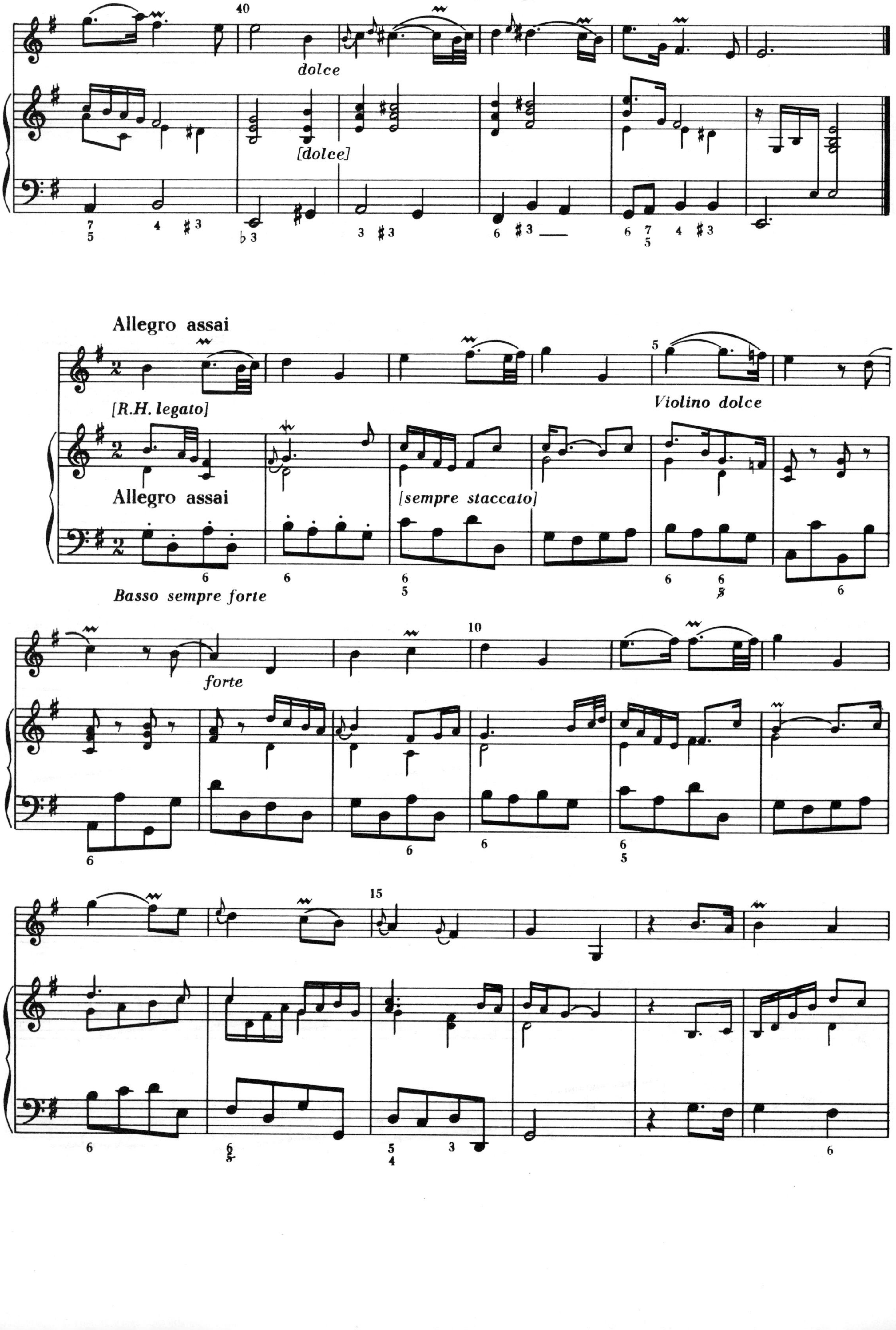

Sonata V

Preludio
Andante, et affettuoso

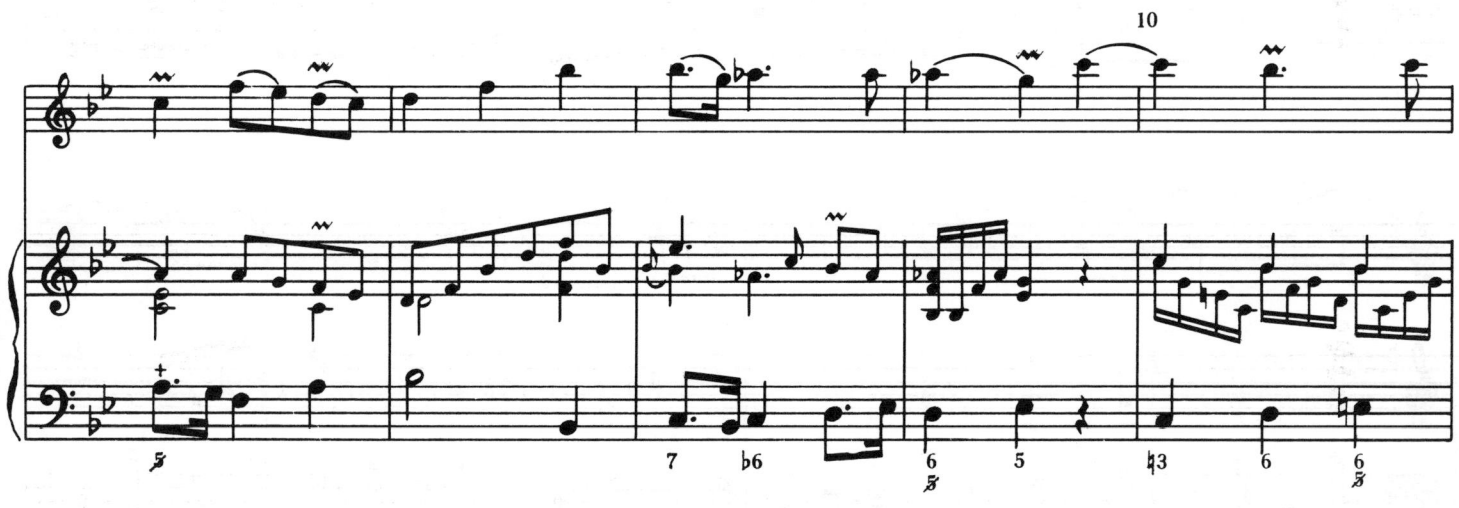

Corrente

Sonata VI

Preludio

Andante, et affettuoso

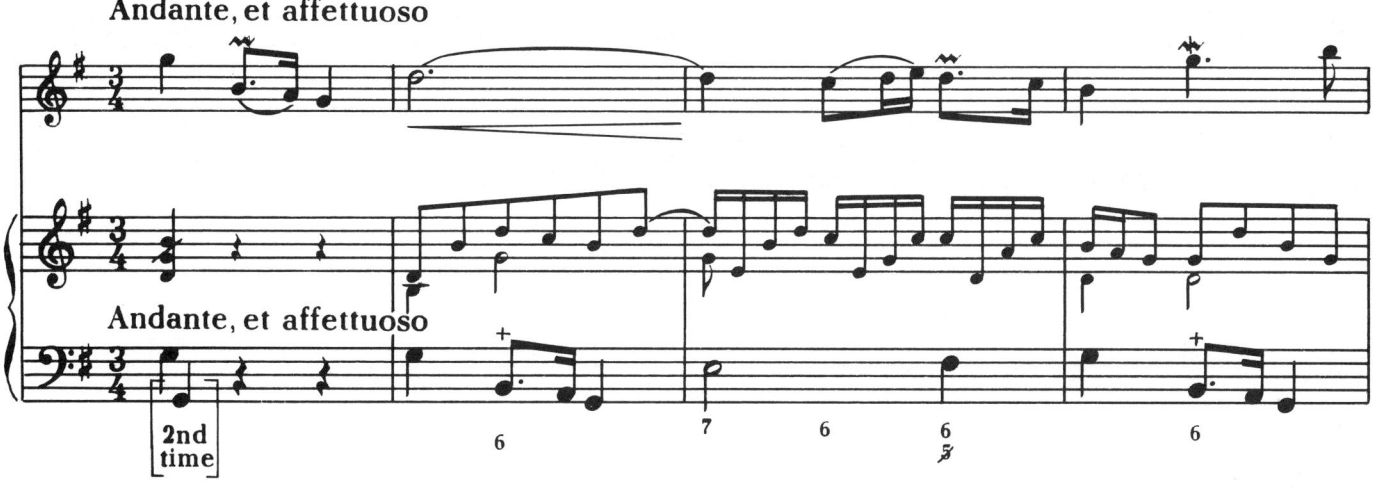

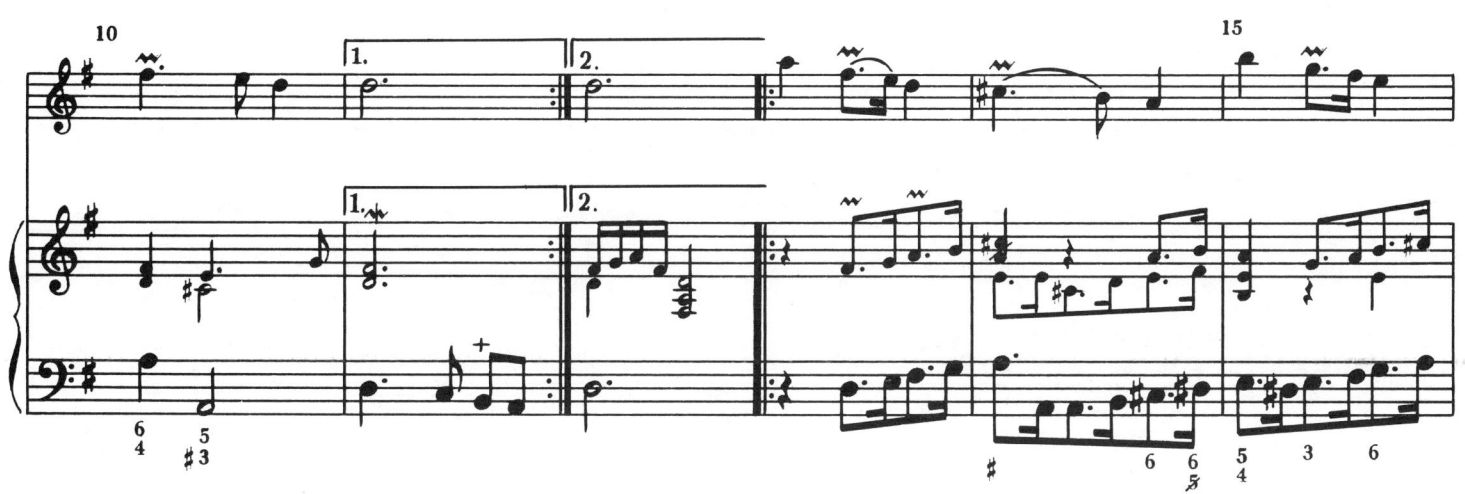

Corrente alla Francese

66

Siciliana
Larghetto

Sonata VII

Preludio
Adagio, et affettuoso

Volti presto
[attacca]

Sonata VIII

Preludio

Grave, e affettuoso

Grave, e staccato

Allemanda
Allegro, ma non presto

80

Sarabanda

Sonata IX

Preludio
Grave, é affettuoso

Allemanda
Allegro, ma non presto

Sonata X

Preludio
Grave, è affettuoso

Corrente

Allegro, é spiccato

Aria

102

104

Sonata XI

Corrente

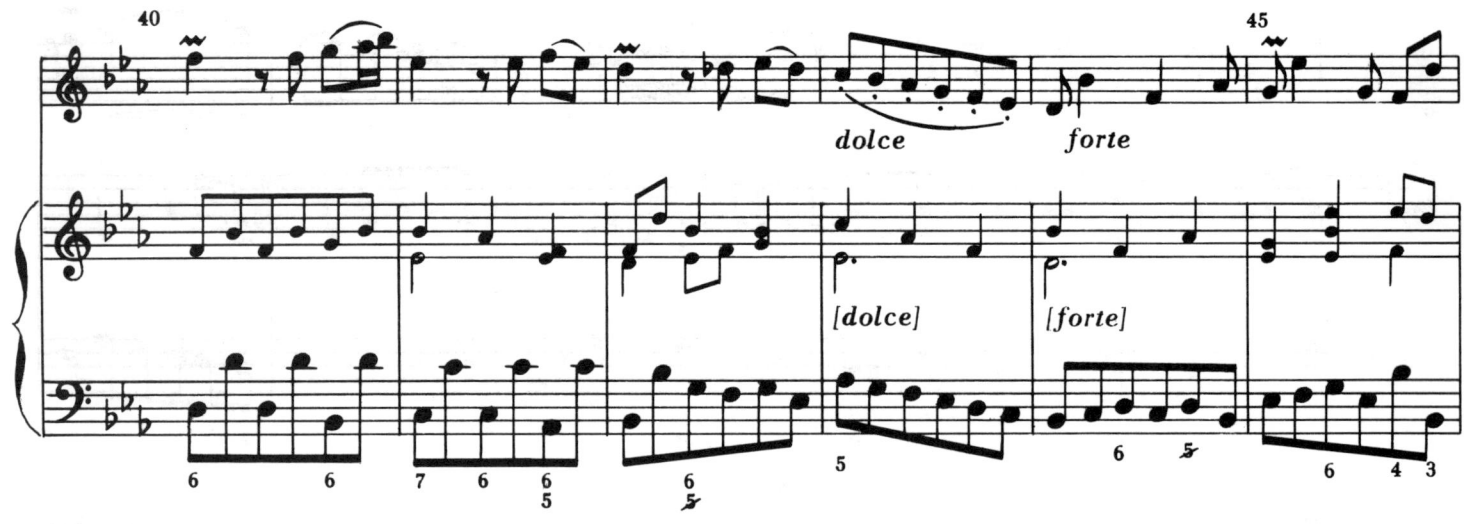
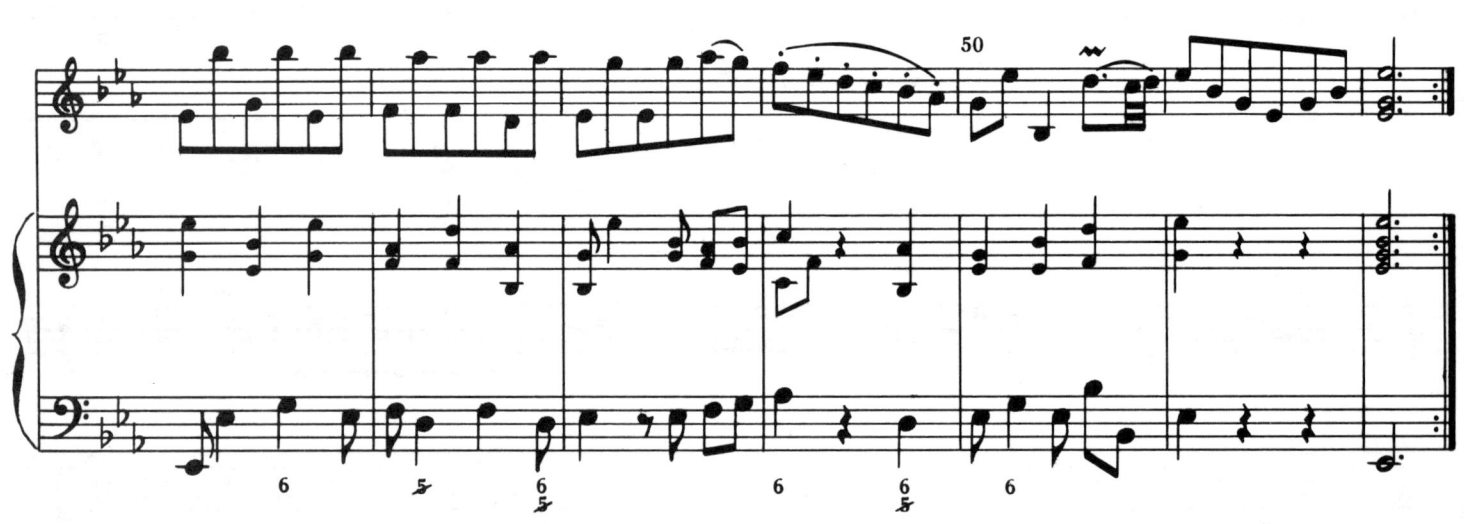

Sonata XII

Preludio

Allemanda

Allegro, ma non presto

Giga
Allegro